Holding It All

Also by Bernice Mennis

Breaking Out of Prison: a guide to consciousness, compassion, and freedom

Holding It All

POETRY OF
Bernice Mennis

Published in the United States
© 2015 by Bernice Mennis
All rights reserved
ISBN 978-0-9885927-8-0

Paintings by Bernice Mennis
Photographs by Ann Blanchard
Cover photo by permission FeaturePics
Book and cover design by the Booksmyth, Shelburne Falls,
MA 01370 [www.thebooksmyth.com]

Dedicated

To our earth whose voice
compels me to respond

To dear friends whose listening
enables me to speak

"The world is too dangerous for anything but truth and too small for anything but love."
— *W.S. Coffin*

CONTENTS

Thoughts on Nature, Birds, Dreams and Meditation

To Hold It All	17
I Came to Your Door	18
Here Is My Poem	19
Wanting to Share With Tired Friends	20
From Tunisia, Dreams in the Day	21
To Live by the Sea	24
What I Thought Today	25
Leaves and Thoughts	27
Nature Fragments	28
Deer in the Orchard	30
Silent Sounds	31
Thoughts	32
While Meditating	33
Ways to Return	34
After Sickness	35
A Bird in the Hand	36
Thrush	37
The Bird Man	38
They Are Birds Too	40
To Help the Good	42
The Worrying Mind	43
The Comparing Mind	45
The Gift	46
On Poetry and Mental Illness	48
Trespassing	51

Questions: War and Peace, Flags and Bumper Stickers

Bars	55
The Passageway	56
Question	57
Other Questions	58

And More Questions	59
On the Theme of Exile	60
Two Pictures: time, place, memory	62
A Walk to the Sanctuary	64
Syria, Three Years of War	65
On Flags and Bumper Stickers	67
Raising the Flag	69
Baskets	71
A Video From Africa in the London Museum	74
Sometimes I Find Myself Switching Sides	75
I Knew It Was a Problem	77
Dogs in Riverside	78

Family Portraits

The Miracle	83
The Wicker Basket	85
Drying Laundry	86
My Mother Repeats	87
Mother	88
Today I Took	89
My Father	90
Looking at My Mother and Father	91
The Piano	92

Lost and Found

A Knowing	95
Lost and Found	96
Finding One's Way	97
Call It the Ice Pond	98
At What Point	99
Lost Again	100
Finding Our Way	101
What is Lost	102
Horses	104
And More Horses	105
A Found Poem	106

Shadow and Light

Building Our House	111
Picking Apples	112
Jogging Past Dave's House	113
Chanukah Lights	114
Playing the Piano, After a Long Absence	115
Spring Songs	117
There is an Edge Within Me	118
To Susan, who died July 21, 2005	120
That Night I Dreamed	121
The Lake at Early Dawn	123
Yom Kippur	125
Another Story	126
The Sound of Longing	127
Memories	128
A Faith I Live By	129
Words Inspired by the Geraldine Dodge Poetry Festival	130
Between Here and There	132
Sounds and Time	134

Fragments After the Fire

Fragments After the Fire	137
Two Weeks After the Fire	138
In the Silence	139
A Prayer	140
I Look for Signs	141
Lost	142
It All Becomes One	143
This is What I Have Done	145
Song, Remembered From a Long Ago Vision	146
To Hold It All	147

Acknowledgments 149

Holding It All

THOUGHTS ON NATURE, BIRDS, DREAMS AND MEDITATION

To Hold It All

Today I felt I could hold it all,
like this shallow stream holding within itself
the reflection of beech, birch, maple, and pine,
and the syncopated sunlight glazing the surface,
ripples of wind moving grass like flowing hair,
and, underneath, the sandy earth and still stones.

Today fifty-five mallards paddle in the moving waters
along a thin edge of ice. Today, I am like a painter
who has finally learned the skill to include everything
her eye can see, my heart often so small, like a thimble,
every little thing tumbling out into the distracted landscape.

Today there is enough space for my continual political outrage,
for Etta singing "Jump into my fire"
and me swaying my own body in the car
to the saxophone and drums,
my hands rhythmic as if with castanets,
and then singing, with all my might,
"And it's all right."

And it is, strangely, all alright this minute,
though a friend lies dying from cancer,
and the terrible suffering of innocents
in the Sudan and the Congo continues,
and tyrants go on and on,
their cruelty oppressing with impunity.

Today there were the ducks,
their green shiny heads and dark eyes,
from who knows where. And how many were lost.
Still the water and my heart could hold them all.

I Came to Your Door

I came to your door to read you a love poem
   by another   but am stopped midair
     by the quiet.
Next to you I notice our cat absorbed,
   licking her entire self assiduously,
     and you reading and writing so intently
       that even my eager blurting energy
         does not disturb the air
           around you.

I retreat and write this love poem to you.

Here Is My Poem

And you said
here is my poem
placing the dandelion by my side.
For weeks we have been blessed
by golden yellow spurts of energy
on fields of emerald green, hundreds of flowers,
thousands of petals reaching out from the center,
the leaves, you say, more full of calcium and vitamins
than all the vegetables we plant,
we weeding out what is most valuable,
poisoning birds we hope to attract.

Now, after the first bloom, you bring
the second, a center dark with closely clustered seeds.
Thin threads reach out into a perfect sphere,
a gossamer flower of soft cotton,
a poem,
exactly.

Wanting to Share With Tired Friends

And aren't we all like that young man at the gate,
open eyed with wonder, needing to tell all casual passsersbys
of the ancient grove of cedars and firs?

So I, deepened by something miraculous,
wanted you to hear the story I had just read
of men at Buchenwald
suddenly brought back to life
hearing a poem in a language
they could not understand.
Hungry, cold, tired,
they crowded around the man
reciting words in a foreign tongue,
and each in his own language
began to touch an ancient script,
the words like water gushing from a well
they had thought long dry.

All I could think,
walking away from our table of polite disinterest,
was that I should have feasted alone.

Life is like that.
No fault or blame.

One needs, at times, to relinquish
shared communion
and be fed by solitary joy.

From Tunisia, Dreams in the Day

It is easy to sink into sand so deep
it is the same as staying so still
that the sand moves over you
and you become part of the dune
or the deepest end of the cave
where the light glows purple
at the furthest point in the sky.
Now I see why they twirl
because the swirl is the same as the still light
in the center, but the heat sizzles it
into a curve, which dances
in the wind like fire.

She rose, her belly arched, her body uplifted
like the dunes blown by the wind,
the source cavernous flowing with life,
the undercurrent beating like the tom tom,
the Berber chant moving along the contour of the mounds,
disappearing into the horizon.
And when you climb the dunes it comes again,
the song in the wind,
the granular texture
velvet to touch.

The women came to the desert to sing
their prayers in the hot sun. And it was good,
the heat was good.   It blossomed
in the wilderness into ripe fruit
bursting with golden laughter.

II
In the village the women came
with their Tozuer black and Kairouan white—
underneath the veil brilliant colors,

under the cloth the naked body.
In my mind's eye I see a film:
"Women in the Hammams before Separation."
Women move as if in a dream, carrying pails of hot water,
steam, haze, slow stillness, silence.
Each woman takes a stone and cloth,
slowly scrubs cheek, forehead, neck,
down legs, down breast and belly,
moving across another—child, sister, friend—
shoulder, arm, back,
stretching across continents.
Water. Steam. Cold. Again and again.
The film is long and slow, like the stretch of pendulous bodies.

Then the women move from that center,
leave hot pool and pulsing navel.
Out from silence come soft sounds—
Arabic, Berber, French, Italian, Yiddish, English.
Over warm and radiant bodies each slowly wraps
bright red and purple, silk saris, velvet pants, dungarees.
Over that, heavy muslin.

Bare feet move slowly out
of separate doors into separate worlds.

III
At night we walk in the oasis
fragrant with jasmine and rose,
citron and orange blossom.
You take the scarf you have carefully wound round
your head during the hot day and hold it out
so I can see how long it stretches in the night wind.
Your long hair dark black and wavy.

On the bridge you begin to sing softly

in a language I do not know, your voice trembling and sweet,
moving through the air like a deep river opening itself
to its own dark swells. In English you translate:
I am an orphan, alone in the world.
I am alone, without father, mother, or brother.
Then you say, it is true, all true. I am an orphan.
And you weep.

I hear in that Berber tongue a Yiddish song
sung by my father of a people wandering alone, without a home,
the voice and the river, the past and the present,
the Berber and Jew becoming one, there,
in the darkness of sweet fragrance.

After the night, in morning light
you do not return.

To Live by the Sea

I have been thinking what it means to live by the sea.
The small wooden rowboat
moving out early in the dark blue dawn.
The men in yellow or black slickers.
The cold Maine waters. The lobsters held in wooden crates.
Rough and heavy ropes pulled into the sea and out.

Farmers, too, before dawn, thick jacketed in mist.
Cows heavy with milk. The ground black, the plowing in.
Hands cold against metal wheels.
And always wind and sky.

In Maine I stare out at houses perched along the shoreline.
Waterfront property hardly lived in most of the year.
Far removed from those who fish the seas.
How often are they lit from within?

I think, I would like to live in those houses
that watch the sun moving on the waters
and hear the waters moving in and out
like one's own breath in the dark and quiet house.
I think, I would like that house.

But it is the one who fishes in the waters
and works the soil I want to inhabit me,
be in me, me as house for that spirit
that lives by what it touches,
becomes what passes
through its hands.

What I Thought Today

What I thought today,
looking at the water slipping down moss green rock,
my eye moving in and out of dark and mystery,
was that I really don't have imagination or intuition
but can see and hear long and wide,
and somehow this fits with my inability
to imagine heaven should someone ask me to
which no one had
but I do remember saying I could not imagine
a heaven more beautiful than this earth.
And that's true.

That's the crux, I think.
All I know is all I know,
which is this world,
its own heavens and hells enough.

When I paint, for example,
I can't just look in my mind's eye.
There's not enough there to inspire.
But, rather, I look out at waterfalls
or light on water or the edge of gold,
the roll of motion and the hazed horizon,
and something gets touched.

With my brush I paint what I see,
the energy stirred by the scene itself,
not quite or only the thing itself
but my meeting it here and now, in this world,
the it being very important
because without it there is nothing
which is why I become so bereft
when I think how it might be destroyed,

can imagine no greater hell
than to lose this heaven
because this is where I reside.

It may be limited but it is all I know.
I can't imagine another place
so bountiful, so rich, so deep, so luscious.

Leaves and Thoughts

The golden leaf, falling from the tree
now curling through the air
now landing in the stream and moving on the waters,
will never return to that branch
cutting across the sky.

Golden birds shake off their wet wings.
Where the leaf has fallen, the pulsating bud.

Clear raindrops like red berries
hang from thin brown tendrils
float in air
drop to the ground.

~

Everything outside me bursts a seed within.
Last night the dark heron silently moving overhead
split into the fiery pink sky that had been gray black for days
and me thinking all birds had already flown south,
and me, now, moving south on the highway.

The pampas grass gray fire, like chimney smoke rising
in front of a glorious dawn, El Greco's steel gray,
shimmering in light, and those two hawks overhead are,
I swear, dancing to Ackerman's guitar.
They must be hearing the same music
moving through my ears.
And now the grass is vibrating with Kitaro's deep sax,
and the blackbirds—ten, thirty—float
like black leaves in the blue blue sky.

~

Radiant, moving like the geese,
nothing, everything, will be lost.

Nature Fragments

And aren't we all gleaners on this earth
looking for fallen fruit left on the ground
when we are hungry,
or a lit house in the distance
when we are lost,
or a fire
when we are cold?

~

Yesterday it was the sudden rainbow
and today the leaves falling gently in the woods
my hands outstretched, my head tipped back
gratitude for all that is given
through no merit
for no reason.

~

If the river is wide enough
jetsam and debris float in light and waves
making swirls of color.
Hard to name what is beautiful or ugly.

~

It is our nature to move the earth
through our own blossoming.
The earth is not just burial ground.
It is sweet soil for rich budding.
Buds are our wings.

~

Don't start with the heavy boulder.
You see those bright colored shiny stones
along the water's edge? Pick those first, feel their warmth.
It is a beginning.

Like a flower
opening to sun and rain
because of silence
the men in prison opening
in that way
because of silence.

~

If I allowed this stillness to move more slowly
I could go into the disappearing landscape of myself.
One yellow leaf lands on my drawing pad
and a few grace my shoulder.
If I lay still on the earth, my body would make a print.
It would be called the place where no leaves fall.

I lie on the rock, full body to the sun.
Cassie sees me as rocky earth, walks over my stomach,
snuggles under my arm, pulls at my jacket,
rubs and jumps and sniffs. I feel honored,
an object in her wide universe.

A butterfly moves in the wind like a yellow leaf staying afloat in the air.
That's me there, afloat and flying,
silently singing the song of unknown birds.

When you first enter paradise move slowly.
You have never been here before.
You may never come again.

~

To meditate this is what you need to do:
Every morning
do nothing
again and again.

I finally got there today by going nowhere very slowly.

Deer in the Orchard

In the morning sun, I feel what they felt in the dark.
Is that presumptuous?
It is the slow sweetness of each step
in a garden of fragrant blossoms, apricot and peach,
where fear has not yet come to disturb the peace.
Silhouetted and barely visible at night,
and now I almost invisible by day,
all of us so quiet, you can hear blossoms fall or open
which they did all night
and all day
in my heart.

Silent Sounds

Silence echoes.
I hear it go on and on.

When the heart is open there are no doors
but still the smile when you enter
a place you can never describe.

If I am silent enough
my mind becomes the book
I would otherwise read.
Words like horses move
across an open field.
The mind had padlocked them behind the gate.
I watch their surprising turns
their sudden emergence
in a far off meadow.
I stand and admire
their grace of movement
within the field
of emptiness.

Sometimes I sit with my thoughts
and they become old friends
I haven't seen for a long time,
grown strange and unfamiliar.
I sit listening
to the rain
outside.

Thoughts

First come the thoughts of all I have not done.
They stay and brew a bitter tea.
Then come the wild turkeys.
They take my heart aflutter
   my mind skimming quickly through high grass,
   perching in a tree nearby, then flying overhead.

They I want to stay, but they move quickly on.

In the open space thoughts of all who have left
   by will or not, they stay still
   in my heart, whether I will or not.

After days of not doing
   there is a cleared space
   by the still pond
   open to receive what will come.

I take this pen and wait.

Now more birds, more words,
more wind moving the branches of the trees,
less preference for whatever moves
inside or out.

While Meditating

Thoughts came when no one arrived at our home
all clean and ready to receive,
you waiting, tired from your labor,
eyes closed, me worried, fearing that all your work
had, perhaps, come to naught.
No one here to receive the fruit of your labor.

And then the thought—no effort is naught,
especially when done in love.
What nourishes the spirit, nourishes the spirit,
it is as simple as that.

The thought continued, with my breath in and out,
you have made our home beautiful,
if no one comes, we are still here,
here is where we reside.

I continued to follow my thoughts and my feet
into the woods, watching the spider in her skillful
and slow labor, thinking it is not as simple as that.
If the spider's work comes to naught
neither she nor her children will survive.
Hunger is hunger, effort is not everything.
We need to eat to survive.

My mind continued to weave.
Still she would knit her web, spinning out from her gut,
as we all do, creating what we need to create.

It is as simple as that
when you are simply meditating.

Ways to Return

You have been away a long time.
   How did your life become so fragile
      that any thing unravels the thread,
         making you start again and again,
           all tangled and helplessly lost?

Watch the cat follow the string,
   the dog follow the stick.

Follow your own footsteps on the dirt road,
   your shadow running silently alongside.
      Listen to foot and heart.
         Let everything lead you home
           one step at a time.

After Sickness

I glimpse grace slipping
into the bathtub, my body stretched out
and open in the hot water
after days curled under blankets,
feverish and sweaty,
spirit having vacated mind and body.

The small tight space of pain,
it's a small corner of a room I hardly know.
Others abide here for years, for a life.

Coming out of the bath,
I feel radiant, almost beautiful.
I brush my hair,
put on a clean shirt,
sit in a chair with a book,

the room so clean and tender now,
everything slow
and filled with soft light.

A Bird in the Hand

A bird in the hand is worth more,
this bird in this hand,
my heart cradling its warm body.
I see her wound
at the vulnerable neck.
She is breathing softly,
her small heart in my palm,
her eyes opening and closing,
she not trying to fly away.
I breathe warm breath, sing oms,
wishing she could fly back to that bush
where she was
before my cat leaped up.

Earlier this morning a nuthatch came to me,
her feet perched lightly on my thumb,
eating seeds from the palm of my hand.

A blessing, to have a bird come to your hand.
This bird, in my hand, at the end of this day,
a deep sadness.

Thrush

Thrush, we think,
looking closely at the bird in our hand
and the book in front of us.

He thought air was everywhere,
not seeing a barrier between this world and the next.

You held him for hours, gave him Reiki.
He seemed better but still could not fly.
I lay him in a small box in my room near the heat.
Later he was gone.
We looked everywhere.

Finally I saw him perched on Buddha
and followed his journey:
leaning against a wooden tapir from Africa,
landing on the wooden flute, its stop shaped like a bird,
sitting among the mushroom birds from China,
finding whatever friendly force he could
in this strange new world,

and, finally, Buddha, sitting on Buddha,
shitting on Buddha, the white tinged with red from his wound.

Buddha receiving it all with equanimity,
and the thrush finding rest there,
on Buddha's head,
as he meditated on the quickness of life and death,
on acceptance, suffering, and liberation.

The Bird Man

It was not so much about birds
but the men who telephoned the man
who knows about birds.
One spoke of the woodpecker who crashed into his car,
the limp body cradled in his hands,
he carrying it indoors, feeding it warm water and honey,
seeing it move its wings, placing it gently near the bird feeder,
then seeing it fly into the air,
the caller, beside himself with joy,
asking the bird man if he did right.
And he did (in his care) and didn't (with the honey),
but it was all alright, the bird flying free.

And the other, a man worried about the birds that had flocked
to his feeder during the warmth of December and January
and were now gone in the cold of March,
asking what happened, worried,
wanting to know they would come back,
the bluebirds, the beautiful cardinals and cedar waxwings,
the robins and one cuckoo.

The birdman reassured him, saying they would.

And the man who called about the white cardinal,
and the other the gannet, never seen before, the black tipped wings,

all so open, caring for life in its tender winged forms,
and I wondered, as I sometimes do,
what it would mean for a young boy to go to war,
which can never be right,
where one sees what was never seen before,
where there is no reassurance of ever returning

or coming back,
to a world or self you had once known,

thought how good it would feel
to heal a wounded heart,
to see flights of bright color return
to a dark world, to feel the flutter
of life in your hand
moving into the open sky.

They Are Birds Too

They are birds too,
but too many.
They chase away the small ones
with bright yellow bodies and tufted heads,
with rosy breasts and sweet songs.
Invading they take over the field,
menacing when they swoop down.

When I look more closely
I see beautiful green luminescence within their black.
They're hungry too, I think,
migrants from somewhere, flying for how long,
looking for a place to stay, to nest, to raise their young,
like any parent, not too much to ask for.

I prefer goldfinch and chickadee,
titmouse, redpoll, nuthatch, cardinal . . .
But who cares what I prefer?

When they fly off together
their fluttering energy excites the air,
the sky alive with motion.
I see a few red winged blackbirds among them,
their bright crimson flashes against the dark black.

I wonder whether to put seeds down tomorrow
for these unwanted ones.
If my cat chased or even killed one,
I fear I might not mind.

Perched on a tree at dusk,
their black shapes are delicate, lovely,
their silhouettes suddenly enchanting.
I rush to get my camera.

What I have judged in others is lodged within me.
I see clearly: anger at beggars circling around,
immigrants swarming across borders,
the homeless, the hungry,
the too many and too much,
ground chucks, squirrels, ferrets, stray cats…
The list goes on and on.

They fly away as light fades.
I watch my thoughts,
my preferences,
my continually judging,
think to make amends
but do not know to whom

or what I would change.

To Help the Good

I was there to help the good
plants have space and sun.
But nothing is that simple
as just pulling up weeds
to allow squash, gourds, cucumbers,
and melons space to wander
at their will unencumbered,
because their will is to interweave with weeds,
becoming fast friends with those I thought their enemy,
their own tendrils searching for any way to travel,
grabbing on to whatever helps in their journey,
as we all do, in unexpected and strangely entangling ways.
And I see how these seeming obstacles provide sweet shade
and how they obscure the wanted ones from predators
unable to distinguish chosen from unchosen.

Not so clear, I think, friend from foe,
he that hurts from he that helps
in ways unforeseen by our best intentions
to protect and preserve, pulling out and cutting back,
now finding I had uprooted what I hoped to protect,
every being so intimately bending to another.

The Worrying Mind

Things I worry about:
Geese flying north in the autumn or, today, already January,
their V's and honks above me in the winter sky;
ducks feeding in a small space of moving water
while all around the ice expands.
What will happen when it freezes
as it has, further up, where a squirrel scurries
across a thin layer of ice?
I worry if it is thick enough to support his weight
or the weight of my worried mind.

And the family which just opened the Indian restaurant,
the clean white cloth and neatly folded napkins,
the sitar playing softly in the background,
and no one there.
And the frame store, always empty when I enter.
Today I bring friends, waiting expectantly for them to buy.

Me, the anticapitalist, worried about dreams and hopes
come to naught, picturing people around a kitchen table,
backs hunched, figuring out all variables,
counting savings, losing sleep, praying,
excited before the big opening,
envisioning happy people coming through the doors,
customers buying goods they've always wanted,
eating the most delicious meal, happy.
Who knows where the mind can take one?

Me, wanting socialism, against exploitation and profit,
knowing we all have more goods than we need,
knowing there are deeper and better dreams,
yet wanting people to enter

the open door of the expectant owners
whom I now imagine as a poor family
sailing through cold winds and empty skies
looking for a place to land, to plant their dreams,
to survive and, with good fortune, to flourish.

The Comparing Mind

I wish I could write like him, those incredible leaps,
I say to myself, surprised at my comparing mind.

I think of a trapeze act,
hands miraculously catching ankles without a safety net
and know that is not me.
I was the first to fall in gym class,
everyone hanging from the bar,
my feet the first loud thud hitting the hard wooden floor.
I have no grasping power, never did.

Not so bad really, I think now,
good for a Buddhist to not cling.

But perhaps I could hold onto one point in the changing universe,
like the poet's apples still golden in late Autumn.
I have seen them, goblets of frozen light in the cold gray sky,
singular, like the beech leaves who hold on
despite wind and snow, their winter leaves transparent,
diaphanous, like death, like life, waiting
until brown husks spurt into green feathered life in early spring.

This holding on of apples in winter—
food for deer, hunted by hunter, hungry,
needing apples to hold onto life in the months ahead.

My heart, too, needing.
Walking in bare woods in winter cold,
I am rustled into warmth by beech leaves waving in wind,
their ability to hold on and wait for spring's new beginnings.

Interesting to start with wanting to let go and find myself here,
touched by the struggle and courage of those who hold on.

The Gift

I didn't know if it were dream or message
but knew it as a gift from a stranger
for no occasion, merit, or reason,
and I trusted that it was good.

And so, as with all that is precious,
I stretch the goodness, unfold each side,
touching the surface, bringing it to my face
and breathing in the air,
fresh like a stream fed by cold springs
cleansed by brown dark earth.
Wrapped in feathered softness
I touch my cat's belly
luxuriating in velvet.

But why me? I have no such softness?

Though today perhaps I am
the woman opening to the gifts the child did not get,
like a field suddenly filled with Queen Anne's lace
    black eyed susans and blue chicory
    goldfinch and hummingbird
    goldenrod exploding at its tip
    like Sam last night at his trumpet
    pure love and struggle.

The bee disappearing
into the primrose is not struggling.
I look at the body moving in its element
of pleasure, color, and fragrance,
this world brimmed with possibility.

I, too, this stranger at the gate,
welcomed for no reason.

I walk slowly into the day
loving my own colors so deeply
I do not know where I separate from sumac and milkweed,
moving so gracefully I am not surprised
to be visited by bird and bee.

On Poetry and Mental Illness

A newspaper article claims poetry heals mental illness
in eight percent of cases.
The researcher does not give other rates—
for drugs or therapy.
And I don't quite know what it means to be healed—
to not be ill, to be "normal," to have ease of well being.
And the exact percentage seems strange,
too specific for something so vague.

But now I wonder, since this is my mind meandering,
my own poem to heal some of my own dis-ease,
what would happen to George Bush and Cheney, Rumsfeld and Rice,
if someone read poetry to them.

The question, though, is not quite right because they wouldn't
or couldn't hear poetry, as they are now.
But let's say they could actually hear,
for example, the words of Stanley Kunitz or Mary Oliver,
Sharon Olds or Billie Collins.
Let me just imagine
since this, imagination, is what poetry most requires.

Stanley Kunitz—they would first not discount
his ninety-seven years of wisdom, would welcome
his small elfish and impish body and spirit.
As he returned to childhood curiosity, pain and shame,
standing in his pajamas on the roof of his apartment,
looking up at the stars, maybe they would return
to their small bodies, return to the sky or the testing tree,
feel again the sting of a mother's angry slap
when the small child, in innocence,
does something which she, in pain, cannot abide.

Maybe they would sense what Kunitz knows,
the power of the unconscious to deepen
and inform with mystery.

And with Oliver, maybe they would see again
heron and turtle, remember the call to mud and marsh,
to sleep under trees and stars.
Would see again the deer as deer, not meat,
the tree as tree, not lumber.
Would love again their body.
Would feel again their place
in the universe of beings.

And with Olds, she is so frank about everything,
maybe they would feel the power of honesty,
not just about sex but about feelings—
something probably so foreign now.
Would recognize the beauty of sensuous layers,
a silken garment, the folds graceful and exciting,
not need to put what is flowing into stiff uniform.
Would feel the joy of surprise by what comes
unbidden in the human heart. Would feel their hearts.

And Collins, they might actually laugh at his playfulness—
the mouse striking a match
and setting fire to a worried woman's house,
the dog howling in an orchestra,
the mind following its own thread
with more than delight, with trust
that one can be led by whimsy
and by reality to something wonderfully funny and deep.

Maybe they would all sit around, nodding their heads
up and down, a smile like Thich Nhat Hanh speaks of,
slowly wending its way

onto their faces, soft and gentle.
Maybe they would feel soft and gentle,
like a spring breeze after a cold winter,
a harbinger of another possible world.
Harbinger, like a bird, a bluebird perhaps,
or chickadee, or titmouse, or a song sparrow,
the song slightly familiar and very sweet.

And maybe each would hold out a hand,
palm facing upward to the sun,
warmed by the sun,
open like a poem,
trusting, holding seeds.

And then the birds would land and eat
from the palm of their hands
unafraid.

And they would be healed, I think,
and so, perhaps, our world.

Trespassing

And if they were there, at the end, waiting for me
to come out of the woods, and if they arrested me
for trespassing on land clearly marked private property,
I would say, in defense: I followed the deer track which led me
deeper into the woods. I made no sound, except praise,
left only two thin and smooth tracks,
went back over the same tracks to not mar
what had been untouched. Paid close attention to tracks
of mouse, squirrel, porcupine, and rabbit.
Listened to the drop of water in the cave for a long time.
I took nothing from the woods,
did not rob anyone,
but it is true that my heart is rich
with unearned wealth.
Yes, I am guilty of walking
in beauty I did not own.
You may take me,
I will go peacefully.
I have been arrested by something large
and have nested in its arms
and am happy.

QUESTIONS: WAR AND PEACE, FLAGS AND BUMPER STICKERS

Bars

At first there were only a few
who needed to be put behind bars
for others to feel safe and protected.
But then the danger seemed to grow,
become more subtle. Frightened eyes began to see
enemies everywhere. More prisons were built
and more. It seemed there could never be enough.
More prisons than schools, more prisons than restaurants,
than apartments in the city.
Nowhere else for the poor and black to live,
no other place to be fed, to be schooled.

Still those few who remained outside
shivered, more and more scared
of the large shadow cast
by the prison walls,
looking suspiciously
at each other,
wanting to be
safe.

The Passageway

At what age does baby turn into boy and boy turn man?
I look at the children huddled together,
clutching their mother's skirt,
an empty bowl, a small possibility of rain,
mother and child hiding from men strutting,
guns slung on shoulder,
walking through the streets
emptied by fear,
young boys hiding who, in a few days or years,
will become those feared men.

What happens to that sweet and fearful boy
still bonded to mother and sister?
What ocean had he to swim
to get to this strange land
where nothing is familiar,
no one family, nothing sacred?
How does he turn into that man?

And is there
any way
for him
to return
to the motherland?

Question

You say there is no way these days
to paint a nude woman and not exploit her,
that is why you put the thin protective cloth
over her naked body or the heavy cloth and veil.

But what would it mean for that woman,
crouched and fearful to move off that canvas
and stretch into herself,
remove the garment and walk naked into the street
clothed only in her own muscular and delicate flesh.

How did it happen that women were forbidden the streets,
their earth, their air, weighted down in veil, suffocated by tight waist,
pinned in with pointed heels and crushed toes?
What would it mean if she rose to her fullness,
walked majestically like a queen,
took back her royal birthright,
took back the night
and the day?

Other Questions

The trembling hare escaping the fox
does not limp back and beg forgiveness.
The arms that tore apart
cannot cradle to wholeness the broken child
who moves through nightmares everyday
yet goes to sleep with the same sweet dream
that this time she will be welcomed
with warm arms and soft heart.

Why do the wounded return
to the source of the wound for healing?
Back to the trap that caught them and holds them fixed,
even when they have traveled far
into the distant horizon?

And More Questions

What are they fighting for,
fighting over,
those men
with guns
while women,
gather water,
plant fields,
cook food
to feed the children,
some of whom will become
the men with guns
who will destroy home and field.

Last night I saw men
with other instruments,
cellos, violins, French horns, oboes, flutes,
playing with love and joy.

And of course it would be insane
for the cello to take up arms against the flute,
the viola to destroy the clarinet,
the piano to silence the violin playing so softly.

Instruments of war,
instruments of beauty,
what we carry,
what we do with our arms
and hearts.

On the Theme of Exile

Each weary and abandoned cat who wends its way
to our window in the winter cold just wants shelter and food.
The last, Pumpkin Shalom, no different from the others.

But those who have come before do not welcome this new one,
though I admonish with words from the Holy Book
to remember that they too were once strangers in a strange land,
exiles forlorn and hungry, seeking simple shelter,
the refrain repeated again and again in the Old Testament.
Someone clearly thought it important.

But still they fight, their own past now invisible in present luxury.
They do not want to hear the pain of the new wanderers.

In the news I see pictures of women
wrapped in brightly colored dresses
to which their small children cling
under the weight of all their lives.
They are fleeing from what was home
to what is not yet known.
A simple hope of safety, an open door.

And isn't that true for all of us?

Yesterday it was the people of Sudan, Liberia, Zimbabwe,
and before that the Congo, three million dead,
and millions of refugees, Rwanda, Angola, Barundii...
Nowhere safe.

And before that the Palestinians, now, still,
and before that the Jews, and before that the Jews,
not so long ago.

What happens to memory?
How can what is so visceral
not touch us, our heart to another's heart,
the feeling of cold and hunger,
the heavy bags, the fear, the fist, the hatred of the other,
the stranger who was ourselves,
who is ourselves?

Two Pictures: time, place, memory

Today I remembered that bearded man standing outside
the butcher shop in Tunis, the words Kosher/Bosher
in large Hebrew letters on the window behind him,
like in the Bronx where my mother and I would shop.
A white apron wrapped around his large stomach,
his arms joined peacefully in front of him,
blood on the apron, a smile on his face.

I remember the smile, the scene familiar,
my surprise that such a thing could be in an Arab land—
a kosher butcher store in the middle of a street,
and on the other side an old and very beautiful synagogue,
chains and locks on its doors,
the guard explaining it was still used
but needed to be protected.
I felt protected.

Later, in the Tunis Museum,
I stood slowly reading
the long history of Jews in Tunisia
when a small hunched woman,
looking like my Aunt Rebecca, approached me,
asking shyly if I were Jewish,
smiling when I said yes,
telling me of the two thousand Jews living there,
her husband, the owner of the Kosher butcher store,
the very man I had just seen.

Today I pictured that man,
as if he had stayed frozen and framed in my mind
all these years, a small Vermeer of another time and place.
Today I worried about him and his wife,
wondered if he were still standing outside his shop,

if the synagogue still stood or if it had been bombed.
I remembered the women in Jerusalem,
the hurried streets, the rush to make their homes spotless
for the holiday, the dirt swept from the apartment above
wafting down, like blown sand, on Raphael and me
as we sipped coffee on his small patio below,
we laughing and yelling up.
That first Passover night, I walked in Jerusalem at 2 a.m.
under the full moon singing, not afraid.

Yesterday another bomb in the large souk near Raphael's
crowded with men and women rushing
to buy food before the beginning of Shabbat.

And everything stopped again

and began again

in Ramallah, Bethlehem, Jenin.
Blood again,
and no one safe,
anywhere.

A Walk to the Sanctuary

It was strange to see reds and yellows fluttering in the wind.
I thought, maybe people are camping here,
washing clothes, hanging them in the sun, on the line, like home.
It felt homey, nice, a family's clothes in a quiet wilderness.

They were Buddhist prayer flags.
A Buddhist temple.

The next day I saw prayer flags on my own road
and thought, how wonderful, here,
in this very community, kindred spirits.
They were red tee shirts, white hankies, and a yellow sheet.

Still, now, wherever I look, I see prayer flags
clean in the wind, the diapers, silk nightgown,
green socks, white underpants, red flannel shirt,
the dungarees, and tie-dyed nighties.
Innocent, vulnerable,
like peace, like prayer,
all over waving,
proclaiming what could be.

Syria, Three Years of War

Do they still take their daughters to school everyday,
their sons with lunch boxes, a sandwich, milk, cookies,
mittens in the winter as my mother knit me every year.
Are there still schools, and lunch, and a way to get warm
in the cold? Do they still get married, make love, have children?
And are there still hospitals and midwives,
treatments for a simple broken bone,
or cancer, or dialysis, or only for wounds from gunshots or bombs?
Do they, like me, welcome flowers emerging in the summer,
daisies and Queen Anne's lace?
Do they delight in the hummingbirds sipping nectar
from bee balm and evening primrose,
and the bright yellow of goldfinch at the thistle?
Do they watch the father woodpecker feed his very large baby,
and the chickadees, rose breasted grosbeaks,
and bright red cardinals move in the air
with the sweet wind and shifting clouds?
And do they wish for rain, as I do, when it has been dry for a long time,
smell roses, locust, jasmine, savoring each flower in season?
Do their dogs run to welcome them home?
Are there beloved dogs that befriend even the most lonely
in their quiet homes, and do they still have quiet homes
and cats that purr on their lap on a soft chair
with a family sitting around a dinner table, passing dishes,
laughing, sharing stories of the day at school or market?
Do people still go to the market for potatoes
or watch the sun set and the dark come,
or look in wonder at the stars, as I did last night,
how they lit the sky in the park?
And are there still parks, concerts, laughter, gambling,
smoking, eating ice cream, singing or sitting quietly
hearing the stream flowing, seeing the light rising
through green leaves as they walk in the woods,

as I did, with my cats, calling each of their names,
laughing as they hid in the tall green ferns,
and pounced and played,
as kids did, for years,
in the years before
the war.

On Flags and Bumper Stickers

The bright stripes on my PEACE flag--
red, yellow, blue, green, and purple—
have become dull by years
of sun, rain, and snow.
And the large silk banner of Earth
suspended between thin branches
and floating in an ocean of blue
is torn, shredded by constant wind.
I wonder how Earth and peace
sustain themselves through the years.

The other day, I took down the PEACE flag
and hung a new one by the road.
A small gesture.
It is radiant, its colors bright
like a child's new crayon box,
especially when the sun shines behind it
and the wind moves through it.
It flows in the air like water.
Cars pass. I pass.
I am happy seeing it.

As for the Earth, I need to take it down
from the branches where it hangs entangled,
need to find a way to mend and make whole
what has been torn instead of complain
about harm that feels beyond repair.

Small flags flutter all around our land,
the Tibetan prayer flags by the campfire
thin lines hanging on a string
diaphanous, transparent, almost invisible in the air,
fragile and beautiful, like life, like death,
like all our prayers.

My car is another story.
It is strewn with bumper stickers,
splattered with mud.
"Minds are like parachutes,
they only function when open,"
and "Sow Justice Reap Peace" can be read,
but "Never have so few taken so much
from so many for so long" is barely legible,
and Voltaire's very true "Those who can make you
believe absurdities can make you commit atrocities,"
was written by an anti-Semite,
confirming that truth is complex
and bumper stickers need to be replaced
with growing awareness.

Yesterday I put on two new stickers:
"Live Simply That Others May Simply Live"
and "War is Costly, Peace is Priceless."

Well said, I think.

Raising the Flag

Is it a duty,
like the flag of Iceland we raised every morning
in the green mist of fog and rain
to show the way for weary hikers?
Or like flags at military bases, a wave of victory?
Or during war, a symbol of endurance,
vulnerable in battle,
sometimes brave, often arrogant,
in the sun beautiful, flowing like water.

This morning, like every morning,
I go to our peace flag, a little tattered
after all these winters and summers of snow and sun,
bravely waving between two maples,
but tangled and twisted by last night's wind,
needing to be unfurled,
to be free to wave its colors
no matter what the weather.

Suddenly I see myself as one of the ancient ones,
praying each morning for the sun to rise over the distant hills,
our chant welcoming the living sun to warm the breathing earth.
Every morning,
because if we didn't…
the consequences too dire,
the responsibility too vast,
who would risk?

And of course I know our peace flag
on our dirt road in the Adirondacks
does not save the earth.
But still who is to say what would happen
if I didn't think it my work

to try in every small way, everyday,
to help peace unfurl just a little,
showing anyone who might pass,
this possibility of warmth
in this world of cold.

Baskets

On the way to the Tucson gem show,
I heard about women of Lesoto and Bangladesh
who sewed shirts, dresses, and shorts,
like Tania's mother and the Eastern European women,
followed by Puerto Rican and Caribbean women,
those waves of women sitting hip to hip,
head and back bent over sewing machines,
the sound of the needle going up and down
and up and down and suddenly stopping
in New York City and Lesoto and Bangladesh,
the doors closed because goods from China
were no longer restricted,
Chinese workers able to make anything cheaper
than anyone anywhere else on this earth.

They spoke of the women who had sewn for five years, ten,
now standing outside closed doors,
having not received their last month's wages,
needing money for food and shelter,
hoping for the work that had already left
their country and would never return.

So when I arrived at the small stand with baskets,
spoons, and jewelry from Indonesia
and saw that what was very beautiful was too cheap,
I couldn't buy it. Too little, I told the vendor, this is too little.
If I paid only this, how could the one who made it live at all,
standing at the gate, her family hungry.

But if I paid more, she would not get more,
and her children would not be full or warm.

So I bought necklaces and spoons
and three large woven baskets glowing like the sun,
russet and burnished and beautiful,
one placed inside the other,
like Russian dolls, round and deep.

When it came time to go home, I carried
the three large round baskets to the airport.
And when I went to the bathroom,
a woman from, I think, the Philippines, who cleaned the stalls,
stopped and smiled tenderly at me and at the baskets,
telling me how she would dry her homemade noodles and peppers,
the baskets perfect for drying the herbs she gathered from the fields.
In Chicago's airport a woman from the Caribbean,
also cleaning bathrooms, gazed at my baskets and smiled,
saying how beautiful. Perhaps she too had worked
in a sewing factory back home.

It seemed every woman of color would smile at me,
now walking so radiant and proud, the bearer of beauty.
At least ten women between here and there
and a small man from Japan, and even a few large white men
who, seeing me try to place my baskets
in the airplane's high overhead bin, helped me, admiring.
And me now smiling demurely, feeling strangely shy
and at the same time magnificent and dazzling,
walking, my head held high, carrying my empty baskets
as if they were filled with precious gold.

And I wished I had bought more baskets
because they were beautiful
and because I could have given them to the women
who were not able to find work in their own country,
who lived here now and worked

in the bathrooms of airports and remembered
home still shining in their eyes.
I would have loved to have given
each of the women I met a basket.
To say, "Here, here,
this is for you."

A Video From Africa in the London Museum

The women were no longer allowed to dance,
so the men wore masks and danced as if they were women.

The children were not allowed to be children,
they became the soldiers who killed.
Now these men, who were these children,
gathered their guns and shaped them into trees,
made of their weapons branches of life.

Here are the artists who were the soldiers,
who were the children who killed,
who now carve intricate forms in wood, stone, and metal.
And here are the women who could not dance
sewing their stories into quilts.

Here were the men with guns,
the children abducted,
the women raped.
Here is their story,
woven into fabric,
a tree of life dancing in the air.

Sometimes I Find Myself Switching Sides

I always root for the losing team
until that team begins to win,
and then I switch.
Problematic to never have your team win,
but my heart, I think, is in the right place
until that place changes.

Like today.
It began with me watching
his huge bulk gracefully moving through frigid waters,
like the seals he sought. But he could not swim forever,
needed solid ice from which to hunt.
In the melting Arctic hard to find a place to stand.

After many hours and miles, he finally reached
a small piece of land where walruses,
hundreds or thousands,
were huddled together.

He slept for a long time, weary.

The more I looked, the smaller he appeared,
his white body almost disappearing on the large white canvas.

When he awoke, desperate with hunger, he tried to enter
the tight circle of walrus mothers and babes.
Of course I am always rooting for mother and child,
her courage and their vulnerability.
But this time, I could feel my heart shift
to the exhausted polar bear, having followed him
for so many miles as he struggled,

his claws not long or strong enough,
despite his many attempts,
to penetrate the walruses' tough hides.

He tried again and again,
then, exhausted and bloodied, gave up,
curled into himself on the snow
and waited to die,
this huge carnivore now looking so small.

My heart went out to him, whom I disliked when he stalked
his own small babes and hunted fiercely, this king of the Arctic,
but, just to say, I never liked kings,
always rooted for the peasants,
he, now, like a peasant, thrown off the only land he knew,

the ice slowly melting
and a way of life slowly disappearing,
and me, on the sidelines and in the middle,
rooting for bounty, for beauty,
for life.

I Knew It Was A Problem

I knew it was a problem when I felt sorry for McDonald's
where I would go for my Paul Newman Organic coffee,
a dollar any size, the best bargain in town I would say
to the cashier, till they stopped carrying it,
"too cheap," she said, when I questioned why.
For weeks they were constructing a new entrance.
When completed no one, it seemed, came,
the lot empty, me actually hoping to see cars lined up
as I did for the man with the garden store down the road,
rows of bright flowers and vibrant vegetables displayed,
Ryan, often drunk, not liking New York City people,
especially Jews, which is exactly who I am,
but still when I saw the rows of beauty,
colors and bounty sitting untouched,
no one pulling in to buy what he worked so hard to create,
I was tempted to go and buy everything,
especially when I saw more and more signs everyday—
50% off all plants, blueberries, corn, Georgia peaches—
the season passing, everyday more plants dying,
and no one coming to buy the labor of his hands.

What is it, I wonder, at my too deep sadness
seeing the small Mexican restaurant,
the father's colorful paintings on the wall,
the bright red table clothes, the smiling daughter waitress
whom I see at the college library late at night,
the tables empty when I drive by?
Or the Thai restaurant, the huge flag "Open"
and all the welcoming signs in an empty parking lot?
And a musician playing (I would say his heart out)
at a noisy bar, and no one listening, except me
wanting everyone to be silent and pay attention.

Dogs in Riverside

This whole idea of ugly and beautiful in humans
resides in such a small field of inches, slants and angles,
distinctions so minute compared,
for example, with dogs,

whom I have been observing all day in Riverside Park,
the endless variation in size and form, the chocolate lab and
white terrier, the boxer and dachshund, husky and Irish setter,
greyhound and retriever and all the infinite and beautiful mutts.

I wonder what each finds attractive in the other as mate or friend,
the precision of smell a sense so foreign to us.

But I was really thinking of the devotion of dog to "master,"
because when I looked at the hill, what I saw were ordinary,
nondescript, freckled and assorted human beings,
all looking pretty much the same, standard people you could say,
except some more energetic and attentive,
others more self-absorbed or passive,
while all about them ran, pranced and played
quite spectacular and unique dogs.

And I noticed how each dog looked so lovingly
toward his own, her own, as if that being were,
how should I say it, special,
the best of the lot.

I wondered if a dog might, occasionally,
cast an eye across a field, noticing another
who, perhaps, threw a ball with more vigor,
or pet with more attention and care.
But I saw nothing like jealousy or envy

or any kind of wanting or comparing.
Instead each dog trotted contentedly, it seemed,
next to her own, looking up sweetly,
tail wagging vigorously, waiting patiently,
that look of expectation and devotion
for the one most cherished and most loved
which, most fortunately, was always the one
to whom she was attached
by leash and heart.

FAMILY PORTRAITS

The Miracle

Each year you say that maybe
next year you won't bother
anymore to make the old foods.
The price of fish exorbitant
the $4 a pound becoming $5
two days before the holiday.
Women bunched together shouting
and then the chopping, grating, mixing.
Hard work for an old woman.
And nowadays, they say, the package
is almost as good, and cheaper even.

Yet each year
there on that clean ironed white heavy cloth
with its delicate stitches of leaf green and yellow red—
I hadn't noticed how small the stitch
how intricate the pattern—
the food there again.
Not simple or quick or fancy
but hours of careful shaping.
It is nothing like packaged food. Nothing.

This year
I was to make tsimes for another seder.
We worked together, my mother and I,
in her kitchen of forty-five years
where the water drips cold
and the hot water never gets
really hot, where the oven
must be watched and the refrigerator
strapped closed.

I was to grate twenty carrots.
And I, the jogger, basketball player, athlete
invested in my woman's body strength,
grated six carrots with great
difficulty, my arm exhausted,
my fingers grated.

And you, my four-foot-eleven,
seventy-four-year-old mother,
grated fourteen carrots
without stopping
not easily or quickly
but calmly
silently

providing again
the dark, coarse, uneven ground.

The Wicker Basket

The wicker basket was old even then, when I was young.
My mother would have me fetch it for her
so she could shorten my skirt, me standing on the step,
chewing bread or thread to not lose my soul,
she sitting on the carpeted floor
while she pinned my skirt, pulling down on my right side,
as if the gesture could make straight what was crooked,
my right hip clearly higher, then and now.
The spools are all there, bright and neat, like children in a row,
all the colors of jackets and hats and socks.
The threads are worn with age, they break at the slightest touch,
but they are lovely. I find her thimble, push the needle through
and smile, thinking this was on her middle finger,
and my sister's earrings, now on my own ears.

I picture my mother bent over her sewing machine,
and at the kitchen table, stitching my black velvet skating skirt
with the red liner, elegant for one who could barely stand on the ice
and walked awkwardly even on the earth.
Remember her asking me to thread the needles as she got older.
Remember watching her careful and skilled stitches.

My stitches are rushed and uneven. I have not inherited her skill
or her patience. Taking the threads from her basket,
I chew on them for a long time
to find my way home.

Drying Laundry

I used to go up there with my mother,
the clothespin bag weighing down one shoulder,
she carrying the basket heavy with wet clothes,
the roof one flight above our sixth floor apartment,
atop the world it seemed, looking out from the Bronx
to the George Washington Bridge
and the Empire State Building.

I'd hand her one clothespin at a time
which she would place in her mouth
as she matched corner to corner
of sheet, towel, shorts, pants.

And when the clothes were dry
we'd hold them against the blue sky
to smell the freshness
and fold the sheets,
each of us coming to the center
of our corner of the universe.

Then the roof was locked
to protect people from drug users and burglars.
Then they bought dryers into the basement for convenience
and added two more washing machines because it was
a long wait, the wicker baskets lined up from early morning.

Then my mother died.

My Mother Repeats

My mother repeats like a litany
the few things that order her now small world.
The important numbers taped to the refrigerator:
Social Security, Mr. Rojansky and the Piaterer,
Joe at the funeral home, the gravestone man,
the friends still alive who should be notified.

She has taken care of everything—paid for the funeral,
the cemetery stone ready except for the dates to be inscribed.
Each time I visit we repeat the journey.
At the bank we sign our names,
walk into a big vaulted room,
and are given a small black box.
We sit at a desk and fold and unfold the few papers—
the will, the insurance, my father's naturalization papers,
a few Israel bonds for education for the grandchildren.

Tonight on the phone she says she doesn't need the vault anymore,
why pay twenty-one dollars a year.
Everything fits into her small dresser drawer in the living room.
Like in her life, she wants her death to cause no trouble.
My mother picks up after herself.
All is neat and in order.
There are no crumbs.

Mother

Your grave was naked, the mound uneven, stones and dirt unkempt,
as you would never be; it was as if you had recently died
instead of it being almost two years since you were buried.

I thought how sad and angry you would be—

And I said to you: mother, I will get a small yew tree
and tend it, as you tended me all my life, caring for my body
with food that nourished and clothes that warmed.

I will buy plants and tend your garden every year.
Give water, prune, take care, as you took care, doing
what you could in the only language you knew.

When you died, the food was all there in the freezer,
small packages wrapped carefully in tin foil and labeled.
I took them to my home far north.

Mother, you are still feeding me.

Today I Took

Today I took your fine Passover china to the antique dealer,
the peony pattern with pink delicate flowers,
uncracked and perfect, a setting for sixteen,
each piece wrapped with care,
thought to sell these dishes and the wine glasses
with their beautiful star cluster.

In the old days, even if you were poor
you had special and precious possessions,
the silver candle holder for Shabbat,
the laced tablecloth for Pesach,
the comforters and wool blankets
in the fragrant cedar chest,
my mother saying, you take this, and I did,
because I loved it.

I took the dishes out, unwrapping slowly
and carefully, to show each unique piece,
my hands chapped and dirty, me in my flannel shirt,
feeling somehow like an old peddler selling my wares,
someone from the old shtetl in the old days,
someone like my father and his father,
riding horse and cart from the small village of Piaterer
through the towns of unfriendly Cossacks
to see if someone might want to buy my wares.

My Father

My father was sick then,
his body hanging thinner on his already small frame.
He had a cane but never used it quite right,
carried it along with him, companion rather than support.
We would walk to Lydig Avenue, from one small stand to another.
He would pick tomatoes, grapefruits, grapes, selecting carefully,
like he always did, slowly, showing me where to squeeze
and where to smell in order to know what was ripe and ready.

As a small boy he and his father drove the wagon
loaded with vegetables from Piaterer to Kiev.
In America he had a small outdoor stand in the Bronx,
with tomatoes and bananas and a cellar to ripen.
At the end of his life, he traveled back
to the familiar fruits and vegetables
and took me, his daughter of thirty-five,
on his journey home.

Looking at My Mother and Father

Looking at them, the cousins, the friends,
I would wonder if all old Jews from Eastern Europe
grew short, under five feet.
It seemed as if this earth that could produce such sweet fruit
had not enough strength for larger growth.
Or maybe it was the uprooting,
the gathering oneself up again and again,
hardly trusting this new possibility of stable ground,
sending only shallow roots . . . in case,
not daring to dig down deep
in what might become a foreign land.

The Piano

I polish with soft white cloth,
my hand moving smooth on burnished glowing wood,
hard wood and elegant, legs delicate, thin and curved,
sitting a stranger amidst a house of rough and knotty pine.
My childhood piano brought from the Bronx
and placed here in the Adirondack woods.
I look at the sun light on the brown gold,
sit down, and slowly touch the keys.
Something deep and familiar is struck.
I see my parents who never touched the white keys
but wanted something they did not have for their children
whose hands would be less rough, more educated.
Now I hear a resonance not possible in that small apartment
crowded with harsh sound. Perhaps it is the high ceiling.
Each note the earth of memory

LOST AND FOUND

"There is a thread you follow . . .
while you hold it you can't get lost"
   —William Stafford

A Knowing

There is a knowing that knows
and a knowing that needs to travel the long way
because already lost that is now the only way.

You look for cairns in the day.
In the night, you focus flashlight on the ground.
There is no moon and feet no long feel their way.

Ancient Hawaiians blinded the children who were to be the seers,
taught them the chants to move through the waters.
The way was to sing the way,
to not look for what could deceive.

But if you cannot remember the chant
or feel the breeze touching your skin,
your eyes strain to see a small island in the immense sea,
and sometimes you find your way home.

Can you imagine what we will become if we embrace all we are?

The long route home, awkward and humbling,
tripping over the debris of wasted passageways
to find our simple thirst and hunger.

My friend will be happy.
I have found bananas and papayas after all these years
and they are good.

Lost and Found

I find them on some disc
and they appear before my computer's eye.
These poems are mine?
I shake my head.
The spirit and feeling slightly familiar
but nothing stirs memory.
I like them, feel pleased
seeing my clear footprints in an unremembered field,
but am disoriented, confused.
Where was I? Where am I?
I have been finding what has not been lost everywhere.

I worry about fires destroying our home
and everything lost,
but these are as lost to me as those would be,
more so, because what is consumed in flames is felt as loss.
I would be there, desperately searching the charred remains,
looking for what was precious,
mourning what was lost forever.

So interesting this other place,
continually finding what was always there,
never missing all that had been lost.

Finding One's Way

The building is familiar, yet confusing.
Too many entrances and exits
in the center of a busy village square.
Easy to get disoriented.
I try to get a clear perspective, to know my direction,
to recognize the door from which I entered
in order to find my way back out,
but I am lost, circling around a turning labyrinth.

In a dream I get a message:
relinquish the need to see clearly
in order to understand more deeply;
relinquish the need to know yes from no,
blue from green, sky from earth,
right from wrong.

I watch the sun set behind the island.
Red moves slowly into blue violet,
the line between water and sky dissolving
in the darkness of night.

I follow the disappearing sound
of the Tibetan bell,
and I am here, in the temple,
all doors now open to the light.

Call It the Ice Pond

Call it the ice pond
    of the heart.
Call it skimming the surface tentatively.
      Call it fear or pain or powerlessness.
Call it not being able to touch any creature
    swimming below the surface,
        familiar or strange.
Call it almost not remembering the summer
      of movement—the beaver's silver motion,
          the frog's surprising spring, the graceful sway of grass.
Call it cold and distant.

In winter fishermen sit for hours on the frozen ice
      before the small dark circle carved by their own hands.
        They wait for the pull on the line.

These words are like that thin line dangling into the waters below
    waiting for something to tug at my heart.

At What Point

At what point do we cease to remember our own forgetting,
act as if who we are now is who we have always been.
And before that point, when we are not yet lost
but choose by our own free will to wander far
rather than lose our self within our own home,
can our loved ones let us go
to our own chosen destination
rather than wrest us back to the self
now becoming a stranger?

Looking out at the layers of mountain ridge,
I can see myself wandering on these familiar hills,
no longer needing to carefully notice where I am
in order to return the same way,
allowing myself to simply go further and further out,
toward sky and night,
a backpack, some water, a blanket
and my own self
intact and in tow.

Lost Again

I think of invisible underground roots
that wend their way for inches and miles,
like the cats that somehow found our home,
stood outside and waited on cold winter steps
for days and nights, or came in uninvited
through the animal door and sat on the chair
in the middle of the room, amid hisses and barks,
patiently waiting to be welcomed home.

All my dream was of being lost
and losing what was precious.
And still in the dream I had the pack I was looking for,
the one with my most beloved possessions.
But it was green, not maroon,
and so natural it had faded
like the mist, into my back.
It was there all the time
holding all I needed.

Finding Our Way

Out of this whole wide world,
how did one tiny green frog with enormous dark eyes
come to this three foot plastic pool in the middle of a dry
and overgrown meadow far from any stream?
And then to have an even smaller one on top of him,
both perched on my mother's aluminum jello fish mold
floating in the pool, surviving the fire
and the journey from the Bronx,
now a resting place for four eyes staring up at me.
And under the hummingbird feeder, in constant motion
the tiny feisty ruby- throated hummingbirds
flying thousands of miles to land here in the Adirondacks,
sipping from small red feeders on our porch
and from the red bee balm, orange jewel weed
and tall yellow lemon primrose,
each plant exactly the right size
for their long thin beaks to enter
to sip sweet nectar.

And me, too, finding this one wilderness to call home,
me, a city girl, now here for thirty-five years.

How we all find our way here and there,
sometimes journeying back and forth,
sometimes staying still, and sometimes
finding enough sweet nectar for all the days of our lives.

What is Lost

What is lost can be found.
Just today, for thirty minutes, I found it.

I looked at tree as teacher and asked what I could learn,
what I had forgotten and would again forget,
and because I asked as a willing child,
tree spoke as a patient elder.

The tops of the trees, broken, the bark wounded and old
spoke not of pain but endurance, shape formed by history,
the not resisting what is.

They spoke of stillness through wind and cold,
the goodness of being unable to flee.
If you cannot run, you dig deeper,
tap something you did not even know.

They spoke of balance from roots deep in earth,
and what it means to branch out,
the horizontal weight not bringing you down,
not falling with the gravity of sorrow or despair,
roots so deep one doesn't falter.

And the high branches spoke in the wind of love
and fierceness, bare branches like locked rams' horns,
intertwined like the violin and oboe in Bach's concerto,
moving in and out of each other, merging and separating,
no preference for a specific shape, nothing seen as deformed,
everything its own dance coming from within.

They spoke of wet sap flowing, how what touches as flow
becomes connection, the body formed and joined forever.

And they spoke, their feet now in high snow,
of spring's coming, their knowing within the body,
their faith that what has been will be again.
They were not impatient.
Winter's hibernation was good, a way to live
by slowing all motion, no need to leaf into sun and blue sky.
The pull of life's energy would come again—
the small folded leaf opening,
the flower, fruit, and seed.
Later the crimson red and bright yellow,
the falling again to the earth,
the going in and under,
the same story.

And I thought, as I listened,
this good news
this difficult news
this same news:
that all will change,
that all will die,
that life will continue

forever and ever.

Horses
Inspired by Joy Harjo's "She Had Some Horses"

She was a high spirited horse, couldn't be tamed,
like to just wander through fields jumping fences.
She would come almost to your hand,
let you think she was tamed,
that you had tamed her,
took your sugar even,
but then, as you tried to mount her,
she'd skit away, moving toward the distant horizon,
as if that were her home,
and it was.

There was another horse there,
would stand in the cold,
stock still,
as if movement meant cold,
as if stillness was a heavy coat
keeping in the little warmth that was left
from the last loving
before the leaving
before the cold got so intense
all you could do was stand and wait
for the sun to come up
and the spring to occur.

Neither horse was ever in a barn,
and I don't know how they got here,
inside my head,
me a city girl
growing up in an apartment,
a thick corral
with very little space
to roam.

And More Horses

She was a speckled horse from another country,
not one of those wild horses that could swim across the waters
but one who kept wandering the dry earth
slowly looking for the home
she never knew
and never found.

The other kept circling, as if tied to a post,
as if stomping the old ground could gather enough dust
to lift her off this earth.
But the rut got deeper
and she never saw that nothing really held her
to that tired ground.

The plodding one knew the stars and how they could guide her
if she would only lift her head and tear the cramping halter,
throw off the rider who rode heavy on her back
and kept her on his track all the day long.
But how and when to make that sudden move
into her own sleek grace.

The swimming horse, she could see the distant land,
the high ragged line of mountain that drew her in,
not like a fish caught but like a woman
who could see her life opening in front of her,
knew where the chord could lead
if only she would follow.

A Found Poem

This is a found poem
of what has been lost,
a history from a page
of a book I do not have
chronicling the lives and deaths of Jews
in seven small villages in Russia and Poland
beginning with P, from Piaski to Piatka.
Page 985.

Piaska, Poland, now Belarus,
Jews present in the sixteenth century.
Two architecturally distinctive synagogues.
The population rose . . . and fell.
On 2 November 1942 children and the old were taken
to the Jewish cemetery and murdered. The remaining
one thousand six hundred Jews were marched
to the Wolkowysk Transit Camp
and soon after deported to Treblinka.

Piaski, Luterskie, Lublin Poland,
Jews first mentioned in 1699. Between the World Wars
Jews suffered from increasing anti-Semitism.
Between Soviet and German rule,
local Poles murdered and robbed Jews.
In early 1940 a Judenrat and ghetto were established.
In March 1942, three thousand five hundred Jews
were deported to the Belzec death camp
to make room for four thousand two hundred Jews
from Germany, Czecholslavakia, and Kalisz
(too many dates and too many places no one knows,
but I am trying to record the simple facts . . .).
In September there were deportations to Belzec.
In October four thousand were deported
to the Sobibor death camp.

The ghetto was liquidated in February 1943.
The men were brought to Trawniki.
All traces of them have been lost.
The fate of the children and women is unknown.

Piaskovka, Kiev. In l939 the Jewish population
was one hundred eighty six. After their arrival
on 22 August 1941, the Germans murdered them all.

Piatek, Lodz, Poland. April 1942 the inhabitants
were deported to Chelmno. (I'm trying to be brief.)

Piatigorsk, Russia. In 1877, the Jewish population
totaled twelve thousand eight hundred and thirty five.
Mountain Jews, called "Tats"
(I didn't know there were mountain Jews)
arrived during the civil war (1918-21)
after being expelled from their villages during a pogrom.
The Germans arrived on 9 August 1942 murdering all the Jews
on 19 September at Mineralnyie Vody.

Piatigory, Kiev, Ukraine (and here is where my story begins
and perhaps I should have started here).
Jews numbered one hundred thirty eight in 1765.
In 1768 the Haidamaks beat and robbed Jews
and murdered several.
By 1897, the Jewish population was
four thousand eight hundred and three
(when my father and his parents and their parents lived there,
carrying vegetables by horse and cart from village to village,
going to the kheyder to study, for generations the same life).
Then in 1926, under the Soviets, the population numbered
(only) five hundred thirty two . (What happened?).
(And the answer): in 1919 the White Army troops
(battling the Bolsheviks) attacked the Jews
(just as my father had feared, leaving in 1917,

posing as the child of his aunt and uncle,
then, years later, bringing over his parents, brother and sister,
who sold fruits and vegetables from small stands
in the southeast Bronx).

On 16 July 1941. the Germans occupied Piatigory
(the Yiddish name Piaterer, the name my father called his shtetl,
the name of the small burial plot at the Beth David Cemetery
where my parents, uncles, aunts, and cousins are buried
and where I visit every fall after the Jewish Holidays).

On 28 August, seventeen males were murdered
(my father, his father and brother might have been among them).
The others were ordered to wear the Star of David
(as my family would have too, of course) and on 26 April 1942,
the young and couples without children
were sent to Buki labor camp.
Ukrainian police murdered all the rest
on 14 November 1942.
(My father would have been buried there
and I would not be here, writing this now.)

Piakta, but it is at the end of the page.
The pages I do not have go on and on.

My nephew returned to his grandfather's shtetl
where there are now no Jews
and sent photos of the Jewish cemetery,
where the Jews are,
along with page 985,
from a book I do not have,
from which I have taken the above.

SHADOW AND LIGHT

Building Our House

During those years of strenuous building
I held up the fragile structure of my mind
insisting it didn't matter if the house fell,
a scaffold I needed to even begin the risk of creation.

When the house was almost done
I dreamt I stood outside and looked in awe
at beauty built through labor of my hands,
loving deeply what I had made.

I woke with fear and knowing.

That morning I looked beneath the house
and saw the sagging joists and knew their meaning:
to love with sharp tenderness the soft flesh and thin bones
swaying over our earth's deep chasm.

Picking Apples

You are picking apples.
We have bags full, all over the house.
And now you are climbing the high apple tree
to reach the distant golds and yellows.
I think why. We don't need anymore.
We can't eat anymore.

And then I see myself sketching Queen Anne's lace,
daisies and black eyed susans,
the dying brown fern curled so beautifully by the pond,
and rocks in the moving waters,
my sketch books from all the springs and summers
piled high in my room.
I think, we don't need anymore.

And the mountain climbed yesterday, Crane,
and only two days before, Sleeping Beauty, year after year.

In the growing quiet
judgment fades.

I sit amidst the fallen leaves
knowing it is these wasteful acts
I will miss most in you
when you are gone,
and most miss in me
when they cease to be.

Jogging Past Dave's House

The first is easier to know than the last,
the last time jogging past Dave's house
to the waterfall, or jogging at all, or walking,
or making love, or opening a can,
or turning the lid for apple juice.
The fragility of the simple breath
lying next to me, the body so small in the universe.
My cat too, curled in my arm, purring,
head cradled at my breast,
I think how long can this go on,
our lives continually turning beyond knowing,
moving into darkness,
and quietly stopping.

Jogging past your house, Dave, I think
how I was going to take you out for a spring drive,
your emphysema keeping you entrapped all the long winter.
It was mid-March, Spring in its faint but clear beginning.

A message on my phone saying, simply, you had died.

Your loneliness and isolation, it would have been easy,
just being a neighbor like you, who offered me wild roses and lilacs
when I jogged by, and sometimes soup during our cold winters.

Passing your empty house,
I think how we never know.

Chanukah Lights

They move to the music
like Mudita's long black tail, sensuous and alive,
like the sea oats on the side of the highway,
like the tops of the white pines today,
the wind outside, the breath within,
the Chanukah candles this night,
the miracle of lights.

The violin and clarinet have kindled my own small flame
and I begin to dance around the room,
my scarf flowing behind me.

Three flames still burning.

When the mind is given space it travels to the heart.

I am there now

with two lights left,

my sister and I betting which would last longer.

I did not think she would go first,
my light both hidden and sparked by her fire.
As a child I would have relinquished
my flame to her. As an adult too, just last year.

There is a soft rain in the dark night.
I listen quietly
and remember my family
driving a few miles north
to see the small Italian houses
shimmering
with Christmas lights.

Watching the candles, I follow where I am led.

Playing the Piano, After a Long Absence

The thought came when I lost the G.
An important note. I would, of course, press down on the key
whenever I read it on the music sheet,
forgetting that it was dead, expecting a response,
and in a way the expectation created the reality.
For awhile I didn't really miss the G,
could hear the anticipated sound
hanging in the air and in my mind's ear.
When the lower D went I felt bad
but reconciled myself with the thought that the B flat
was more important in most pieces I loved,
which was true, except that then it, too, went.
Losses are not contained, they continue.
Soon whole sections of music stood silent
though my fingers continued to press
the flattened unresponsive keys.

I would occasionally remember the weaker notes
and press a hard and heavy finger down on delicate white.
Sometimes it would sound. But in the gesture
what was sweet and soft was lost,
and in the waiting for the note to slowly rise,
rhythm and spirit sunk a bit. Still there was enough.

Today, in this hot and humid summer,
it's even worse. More notes lie fallen.
I picture a battlefield. It's just loss, I think,
and wonder how much of any life can be lost with spirit
staying intact. At what point, I questioned,
while playing a diminished Pachelbel,
do we despair and stop playing?
How much imagination can fill how much empty space?

I continued to play and thought of Beethoven,
stone deaf and still he could hear music within his mind's ear,
could create whole symphonies. It's clearly possible.

That's the key, I thought, still playing and coming
to a particularly beautiful section where everything seemed
suddenly whole. To hear the deeper notes that still resound
within us, no matter how much is lost.

And the more I played, the more limber my slow fingers.
The G actually returned.

I thought of my travel cross country with my first tape recorder,
my companion unable to hear through the muffled sounds.
But on that whole long trip,
I sang along with Emmy Lou and Janis, Joan and Dylan.

What can I say? I knew the music and I was happy.

Spring Songs, like the Song of Solomon to the Beloved

Digging up the old plot, I see carrot sprigs green and alive.
What I forgot last Autumn comes up this Spring,
crooked and crow footed beings,
orange and bright, they taste like the woods,
old beings who have been in earth a long while,
more like trees than plants. Survivors.

I nearly cut down the bare branches of spirea, dead and brittle.
This morning, tiny spots of green,
which, in my haste, would have been lost.
The seeming dead, you never know the life within.
Locust, I remember, always late in their green,
their spiked dead branches, the brown dry pods,
suddenly burst into clusters of white peas,
sweet and fragrant, luscious, like grapes.

The memory of what was tells me what will be.
It's important, I tell my students and myself, to know history,
to not presume from external appearance
what is or will be possible.

Michael, in prison so many years, a dry seed in a hot desert,
how could he presume, yet he did, to grow.
The water of this school—all its strange and beautiful blooms.

He said, at graduation,
I am not who I thought I was,
I am who I am,
and it is not who I was.

There is an Edge Within Me

The last day of ten days backpacking
in the Pasaytens in Washington
the trail just disappeared and there we were,
on the cliff, looking down, knowing that somewhere
out there, where the river ran,
there was a trail.

So we slid down the rocky slope to the river
and when the river ran too deep and fast,
we would climb the cliff until we could go no further,
the edge too precipitous for my shaky feet.

Down and up, again, and down, again,
and honestly I thought I would never get home alive,
and so began to tell you what to tell
my mother and partner and friends,
assuming you would, somehow, live to tell the tale.
Thank them, I said, for this good life, this good death,
and I meant it.

But the edge that surprised me was not the hard edge of the cliff
or the shaky edge of fear, but the soft space in my heart
during those days of near death.

That first night of the lost day,
when we finally found a small ledge to lay our tent,
I, seeing the green spring grass move so softly,
fragile grace in the mountain wind,
could not lay down the tent,
too sweet and vulnerable this grass of all our lives.

And when I slid down the mountain and saw blackberries,

I grabbed the thorny bush, not to stop my too quick descent
but to eat of the berry.
If it were to be my last day, how could I not partake?

During those days
I was better than I thought I'd be,
grateful for grass and berry
and touched by everything I touched.

To Susan, who died July 21, 2005

It's not that I think the world should stop because you have,
much sooner than you or I wanted or expected,
but still there is something strange about everything moving on,
especially me, as it will, after we have gone
because that is the nature
of life and death.

You know the question whether a tree falling
in the woods makes any sound if no one is present?
I think of those ancient white pines our neighbor cut down
without our hearing their death, we finding them
lying on the ground, the resin still flowing,
their large presence no longer guiding
my everyday walk through the familiar woods.

When something immense dies
surely the empty space should resonate the loss.
And so I want the woods to resonate your death
and the stars and the birds and everyone I know to note
this passing of an immense and precious presence.

I remember the first play you were in.
I, young, eager and anxious, waited for your part,
knowing your lines would come when the curtain first opened.
People were still talking casually to their friends
as if nothing special were about to begin.
I wanted that hush in the world
so all could feel your entry, your first words,
how those words were the essential beginning
and how, without them, it would be
very hard to ever understand
all that would follow.

That Night I Dreamed

That night I dreamed my sister was all adazzle,
dancing and beautiful. And I thought, sadly,
doesn't she know she's dying? And when I awoke
I thought, don't we all know we are dying?

After days of darkness and cold,
the electric power lost in the storm,
the lights came suddenly on. The first sign the blue,
green, and yellow Christmas lights on the dark spruce,
and the white lights on the small plastic wire deer
grazing in front of the tree. I had meant to turn on the light
under the house to warm the pipes I feared would crack
when frozen water began again to flow.
I had made a mistake. I was glad.
The joyful colored lights, I need to remember,
not the practical or needed but the dazzling,
because my sister was not practical at all,
shimmering with brilliant color, lighting
the darkness and bringing warmth.

I think of gestures that seem foolish,
especially if one knows one is dying.

My sister gently rubbing expensive cream on her face
to keep at bay the aging wrinkles. An illusion, I know,
especially two weeks before her death.
And Sadie, a huge just found bone in her mouth,
prancing joyfully in the field, searching for a place to bury
the treasure to feed her future hunger, although she died that week.
And my old sick cat following the ratty string around the carpet floor,
jumping in the air and then hiding under a chair waiting expectantly
for me to put down whatever I am doing and find her. And I do.
The cardinal flinging himself every morning at the window

battling his imaginary enemy who looks exactly
like his own very beautiful red self.

I think of the love where you and the other know perfectly
the truth of an illusion, yet both continue the deception which affirms
beauty, play, courage, and dignity in the face of the death
that both know will be.

What I need to know is that this world
is not the work of a practical utilitarian creator.
Just look at heron and mouse, lily and lizard,
artichoke and armadillo, and the snow
now sitting atop the bud
and lining the soft branch
of staghorn sumac.

The Lake at Early Dawn

In the early dawn
I row toward the rising sun
to reach the remaining mist
at the far end of the pond
before warm touches cold
and mystery disappears
into water.

From the corner of my eye
I see the loons for whom I have searched.
Have they been created through my longing,
a mirage disappearing when I turn my boat?
They slip under water
and quietly disappear
with no trace.

I move toward dark figures at the far end
who become, as I approach,
what they always were: rock on top of rock.

Suddenly two loons appear by my side,
their dark black heads,
their patterned intensity of black and white.
One begins to rise, a ballerina,
with webbed toes touching water,
wings outstretched into air,
she of both air and water.

Their cry of longing in the air,
like my gaze into the distant mist,
disappears and comes again, and again.

I row far out to see the mountain
I know is there and take comfort

in what is unchanged.
I think of the one I love,
wishing her here, by these waters,
hearing the sound of loon,
seeing the mountain
lit by the rising sun.

And I think of my sister,
no longer here on this earth,
how she loved birds, in nest or flight,
and loved the sea.
I see her swimming,
her small strong body
moving beyond my vision.

I know our beloveds are immortal
in heart and memory,
but today I feel their presence
in all they have loved,
how each time we who still walk this earth
and swim these waters see what was loved
we remember the one who loved,
a mystery within and beyond our reaching.

Yom Kippur

This is the beginning of a poem a day, a promise.
May it be here, where I have taken pen to paper
to remember the leaf I caught while jogging and let go,
like a too small fish, like a too large treasure
for my small grasping hand.
May I remember the letting go.

This is the day after the evening of Kol Nidre,
when we ask forgiveness
for promises we will not keep
in the year to come,
those bright leaves of poems not written
and hopes that fall with the leaves on the road.

Knowing all seeds will not come to fruition,
God, on this holy day, forgives us before we fall,
understanding the pain when effort and intent
miss the mark, as they often do,
knowing the discouragement of heart
that wants and hopes but cannot always do.
The kindness of forgiveness
before the sin.

Another Story

Very cold, the wind harsh,
I think of refugees, in thin tents,
on cold mountains for days, years,
or the homeless on city streets, a bench,
a warm vent, hiding from the police,
and yesterday, the small black cat running
in front of my car into the deep snow.

And then, for no reason,
I thought of Jesus suffering on the cross,
a fate both chosen and unchosen.
But not him alone, the other two suffering beside him,
each on his own cross.
Forget that the other two were guilty,
who knows even if they were,
and if it were robbery, who knows why,
possibly to feed their family or get a doctor for a sick child.
But even if there were no good reason, to be killed for robbing
is too much, and too cruel, especially on the cross,
the common punishment for all crimes in those days.

And I wondered what it would mean to have a different story,
three beings on the cross, a multitude through history,
and a religion large enough to include all
our utterably painful and joyful
lives and deaths.

The Sound of Longing

The sound of longing
traverses the miles
of separation.
It is the cows,
their babies taken away,
not yet for slaughter
but for fattening in greener fields.

Brought down from the hills
they are put in locked barns.
Otherwise they would jump any fence.

We hear their bellows in the wind,
that deep sound of distress.
One head strains over the barricade,
another squeezes into a small crack in the old wood.
Joe says in a few days they will forget.
Forget and remember all that is lost
and is no longer.

People speak of war, competition,
greed, hatred and ignorance,
as our human condition.
I think how we, animals, risk lives to save our young,
build nests and feed, circle together to protect,
bellow through green fields for days and years
for children taken too soon,
for all that has been lost.

Memories

Enclosed in mist and surrounded by water,
something in me rises to the surface.
A small child, almost invisible, her head peeking around
a wall, waiting and wanting to be welcomed
into a room of laughter and warmth.

She is not asked in.
She waits for sister or mother to say,
come in, come in.
But the words do not come.

Now, in the doorway,
her friend blocks a man reciting a poem
she wants to hear, she in love with its sound and rhythm,
she smiling at the table,
sitting with her notebook,
he not invited in, she not asked over.

This strange familiar longing, here in Iceland,
far from the small child in the Bronx.

Memories come unbidden,
like the sheep to this porch
on a night of cold and icy wind.

Feelings move on dark waters.

The driftwood lying along the shores
of the fjords of Iceland,
come, it is said,
all the way
from Russia.

A Faith I Live By

Not the second coming, this is a rapture from the earth.
It is a faith I believe in because I know
what it means to be lifted by beauty,
above the tall pines, their needles glistening with morning light.

This is a faith I believe in because I know
the shadow of darkness moving under the white light of ice.
Above, the tall pines, their needles glistening with morning light.
High and low reflected here, no way to separate heaven from earth.

The shadow of darkness moves under the white light of ice,
its edge like fine lace from the old country.
High and low reflected here, no way to separate heaven from earth.
The rapture to be wrapped in a cocoon of love
transported into darkness.

The thin edges like fine lace from the old country,
not a second coming, this is a rapture from the earth.
The rapture to be wrapped in a cocoon of love
transported into darkness.

What it means to be lifted by beauty,
this is a faith I live by everyday.

Words Inspired by the Geraldine Dodge Poetry Festival
(some might have been stolen; I was in a state of love)

If I get myself out of the way
who will be left and what will she say?

Can I translate myself into the original?

What is denied us:
in the third grade told to not repeat a word
in the second how to draw a snowman
before that things said about the body
the message unclear but the tone exact.

We could go further back
to when it began
the unraveling of the love,
the covering of the light.

How does the spirit return to the body?
Confusion opens a channel to the soul.

I'm imbued in the fabric of things.

Everything is contagious. The question:
what we want to catch and pass on
and what we need to protect ourselves from
because there is danger, those murderers
dressed in sanctimonious clothes.

What was said to the rose to make it open,
to the cypress to make it strong,
to the jasmine to release its fragrance
and the sugar cane to make it sweet?
Whatever was said, the spring began to flow.
The people in the town heard something
and that is being said to me now.

The great warehouse is open.
It is all happening here, in my chest.

Every poem is a lullaby,
so sleep, child, sleep.

I am a child again,
open to everything in the world,
bursting with joy. Except the person in front of me
gets angry at my blue raincoat touching her chair
and my excited foot beating in time.

I close up

but I open again,

refusing to relinquish to another
the fullness of my possible self.

Love abounds, love abides.

Between Here and There

Between here and there
worry and hope
desire and fear
imagination, consternation, presumption,
a landscape of the continually fading into the distance
of nowhere now.

But now the magnolias and cherry blossoms,
bloodroot, hyacinth and daffodil,
violet and trout lily.
I bow down to the wild lily of the valley
and praise the earth of continuous birth.

The hellebore, a tiny spear in late winter woods,
now a spreading fountain of spiraling green

which will be gone
as will we
soon enough.

I take the leeks and wash them in the stream
and make a soup with potatoes.
I pick the spinach and the red leaf lettuce
and the leaves of the spirited dandelions,
spreading everywhere on this sky of green,
returning each summer despite the arsenals
of anger raged against them,
our desire to control what we do not want,
the neat and cropped lawns absent of the curls of life.
But they survive, and flourish, with the coyotes.

Why choose death now,
here, in the midst of this life?

We will, we know, all be there,
soon enough.

Sounds and Time

The slow engine of my Cassie's continuous purr
touches me as I touch her.
The tick of the clock, the minutes passing,
and the woodpecker's steady beat.
The cardinal every morning greeting himself at the window.
I think he is saying good morning.
And the chimes, a small church praising the wind,
each day a different hymn.

The tick of the clock is even, as is the woodpecker's steady beat.
I scatter black seeds everywhere for my sheer delight.
The chimes, a small church outside my window,
praise wind and world, every moment a different hymn.
I do not know the song, but still I am called to worship.

Black seeds scattered by my own hands
every morning for my own delight.
And today the sun shines. I move my small stool to be in its light.
I do not know the song but how could I not worship
this world created from seeds beyond my imagining.

Today the sun shines in the window.
I move my small stool to sit in its light.
The slow engine of my cat's continuous purr
touches me as I touch her.

This world is created from small seeds
scattered by my hands, beyond my imagining.
The cardinal every morning greets himself,
or is it me,
to whom he sings?

FRAGMENTS AFTER THE FIRE

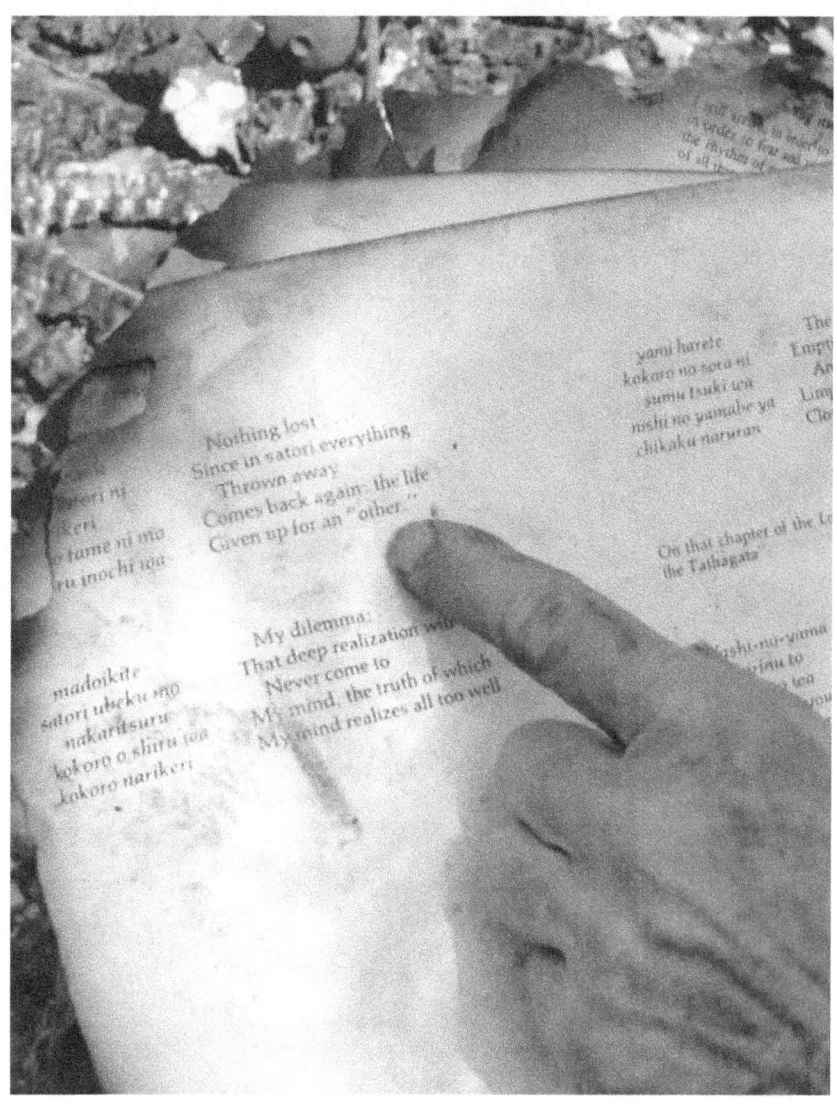

Fragments After the Fire

Hard to separate what is wet and charred—
a skill to not tear what is already scarred and torn,
to save and not damage,
to savor the remnant that survives—
a few words, some sheets of music,
lines of a poem,
a piece of a sketch.

Why save this
and what was this
and what can I be now
and how to mend parts to make whole?

I have found ink drawings of a camel
and Ali, in the desert of Tunisia,
and the story of the synagogue in Tunis
and the women in the hammams.
Should I trust what was most precious will be found
and what is not found will be remembered
and all I have is all I need
which is what I have always believed?

Yet this strange joy in finding one camel
on one page
from one journal.

Two Weeks After the Fire

Crocuses pop up suddenly,
yellow, lilac, white, tender.
Golden yellow coltsfoot tickle my path
and wave by the stream.
The spring flows out from rock and dark earth,
around it purple periwinkle and deep green leaf.
Forsythia and magnolia are in bud.
All is not lost.

Looking out
I see bright white blossoms,
sweet the fragrance after breathing ash,
raking and sifting loss.

I take one blossom to travel with me.

In the Silence

In the silence of loss everything speaks.
Scattered poems, forgotten, now appear.
Pages empty of print tell stories.
All that we had and for years never saw
emerge now from the ashes,
phoenixes, every page
saying I am here,
pay attention.

~

With no home the guinea hen
huddles by the car
to catch the early morning sun,
warmth she would get from the light of the porch
of the house that is no more.

We all find our way.

A Prayer

A prayer of gratitude to what was.
To what was lost.
To what was found
 amid all that was lost.
To all that can grow from loss.

After the rain last night,
after so much dust and dryness,
the flowering again.

To all that was and still is
and will be
Thanks be
Thanks be.

I Look for Signs

I look for signs of life.
The tiny red maple leaves suddenly appear on two branches,
the rose vine cascades under the wood pile,
the azalea spurts small green leaves.
I find Tania's cup and broken plate, buried in ash,
the crushed metal merry-go-round,
paintings and sketches, torn, parts missing,
almost beautiful in their new forms.

I handle each piece reverently,
place them delicately on the earth,
as if they are the treasure they are,
this small remnant, even the porcelain fragments
almost unrecognizable,
the warped and twisted metal,
and me seeing anew, defining again,
what is precious, what is life.

~

This morning I breathed sweetness
and didn't smell ash.

After the fire I knew our loss could be comprehended,
was not measureless, like mountains, rivers,
aquifers, springs,
like air and earth.

Lost

Today I thought
it is not always good to find what you have lost,
to be reminded of those who are gone and already buried.
My sister, seven years ago, finding the obituary,
the cards, the list of friends, the last picture
of what we thought would be the last chemotherapy.

I keep finding more and more pages
of *Image Before My Eyes*,
more than one book could possibly contain,
images too painful, page after page
I want to stay buried
with all that has been lost.

It All Becomes One

It all becomes one,
the particulars of piano, table, couch, poetry,
now ash and indistinguishable.
Compost too, red tomatoes and green pepper,
lemon and grapefruit, egg shell and corn cob
now dark rich soil.
And all that comes into us . . . and out of us . . .
all that was individual and distinct,
this process, this ash, this oneness.

Why do I find these dishes I never liked everywhere?
Why this one kokopelli earring I never wore when there were two
and all the loved ones gone?

I dig and scavenge for the precious that should have survived:
the singing bowls, Tibetan bells, my mother's mahjong set,
the graceful teapot from Iran.
The lesson about the wanted and unwanted
and what is found again and again amidst layers of loss.
How you can't look for a specific beloved,
my father's sterling silver cup brought from Russia
for wine for the Holy Days,
or the photo of me looking up at Susan,
my questioning hand and loving gaze.

Still what survives asks to be seen,
survivors, even those we do not want,
we wanting the other who is not there,
the most beloved child, although we would never admit it,
especially to the one still there,
scorched and stunned and in shock.

Not easy to be a survivor amidst all who have perished.
My Uncle Jay, a survivor of the Shoah,
when asked how or why he survived the camps
said simply *bashert,* fate, no reason why this and not that.
"Abide," Kevin's word as he lay dying of cancer and in pain.
"Relinquish," my word, digging through the ashes
of what was our home.

I find a small wooden *zeyde* and expect
to see *bubbe* next to him,
and next to both that silver chalice,
next to what was the piano.
Instead I see photos of Nazis, children with arms raised,
death camps, resistance fighters, yellow stars...
almost every page from *Image Before My Eyes,*
the history of Eastern European Jews, all intact,
a strange miracle, this survival of all that has been lost.

I gather the pages drying in the sun
and relinquish this, too,
the desire to share something deep and incomprehensible.

Abide and relinquish, two words to live by,
and *bashert,*
and the challenge to live
with all that remains,
with all that was lost.

This is What I Have Done

This is what I have done these days
and this is what I have found
and it is nothing new
but it is all new
because lit in a dark sky.

~

There are diamonds in the coals.
To see what is precious you need what is charred,
what holds history under pressure,
coal turned now to diamonds.
You need darkness.
You need to not be encumbered
with light and grace.

~

All that I gave away was saved.
All that I saved was lost in the fire.
All my possessions lost.
All I possess with me still.
Inviolable.

Song, Remembered From a Long Ago Vision

I am the doer
I am the giver
I am the earth
I can receive.

I am the sunlight on the mountains
I am the shadow under the trees.

I am the bird that's in that sunshine
I am the snake that's in that shade
I am the bird that sings so softly
I am the snake that moves so still.

I am the wind whose music dances
I am the earth that makes no sound
I am the sound that turns to silence
I am the silence that can be heard.

I am the roots that go deep under
I am the boughs that sway so high
I am the old one who seems to foolish
I am the child who seems so wise.

Sometimes I know my life's a circle
always flowing returning home
but something I feel I have no center
I am a spot lost and alone.

Then I go to my own mother
touch her earth and breathe her air
drink her water, see her bounty,
and I know my heart is there.

And I know my home is there.

To Hold It All

Today I feel I can hold it all,
like this shallow stream holding within itself
the reflection of beech, birch, maple, and pine,
and the syncopated sunlight glazing the surface,
ripples of wind moving grass like flowing hair,
and, underneath, the sandy earth and still stones.

Today fifty-five mallards paddle in the moving waters
along a thin edge of ice. Today, I am like a painter
who has finally learned the skill to include everything
her eye can see, my heart often so small, like a thimble,
every little thing tumbling out into the distracted landscape.

Today there is enough space for my continual political outrage,
for Etta singing "Jump into my fire"
and me swaying my own body in the car
to the saxophone and drums,
my hands rhythmic as if with castanets,
and then singing, with all my might,
"And it's all right."

And it is, strangely, all alright this minute,
though a friend lies dying from cancer,
and the terrible suffering of innocents
in the Sudan and the Congo continues,
and tyrants go on and on,
their cruelty oppressing with impunity.

Today there are the ducks,
their green shiny heads and dark eyes,
from who knows where. And how many were lost.
Still the water and my heart can hold them all.

My Gratitude
to

All my good friends through the years,
in particular those whose words
appear on the back cover

Marian Kelner, for her close, perceptive
and very helpful feedback

Ann Blanchard for her years of loving support

My family whose presence continually
dwells within me

Colophon

This book was composed during
the chilling Winter of 2015
using the warm and graceful
Minion Pro, an Adobe Originals
digital typeface designed by
Robert Slimbach.

∽

www.ingramcontent.com/pod-product-compliance
Lightning Source LLC
Chambersburg PA
CBHW022116040426
42450CB00006B/728